All the Good
Leader Guide

All the Good:
A Wesleyan Way of Christmas

All the Good
978-1-7910-1797-2
978-1-7910-1798-9 eBook

All the Good: DVD
978-1-7910-1802-3

All the Good: Leader Guide
978-1-7910-1800-9
978-1-7910-1801-6 eBook

All the Good: Devotions
978-1-7910-1809-2
978-1-7910-1810-8 eBook

All the Good

A WESLEYAN WAY
of CHRISTMAS

Laceye Warner · Amy Valdez Barker
Jung Choi · Sangwoo Kim

—•— LEADER GUIDE —•—

by Sally Sharpe

Abingdon Press | Nashville

All the Good
A Wesleyan Way of Christmas
Leader Guide

Copyright © 2021 Abingdon Press
All rights reserved.

978-1-7910-1800-9

21 22 23 24 25 26 27 28 29 30 — 10 9 8 7 6 5 4 3 2 1
MANUFACTURED IN THE UNITED STATES OF AMERICA

Contents

To the Leader

Advent invites us to anticipate, receive, and respond to God's amazing love embodied in Jesus Christ, and the purpose of this unique Advent study is to help us do this in a "Wesleyan way." For John Wesley, the marks of Methodism were not religious opinions or doctrinal commitments but the acts of receiving God's love in Christ and responding by practicing love through holiness of heart and life. Drawing from practices encouraged by disciples throughout Christian tradition, Wesley emphasized practices of piety and mercy, or good works, which often are referred to as means of grace. So, in this study you will walk with a group of participants through the four weeks of Advent by reflecting on biblical passages and Wesleyan themes in light of various means of grace. The four chapters explore the themes of

1. practicing Advent (preparing the way),
2. practicing prayer,
3. practicing mercy and care for others, and
4. practicing God's mission to the world.

As you make your way through the study, allow the following two questions to set the tone and overarching framework for all that you do and discuss in your group:

- What would it mean for us to understand ourselves as *fully* loved and accepted by God?

- What does it mean to accept God's grace in Jesus Christ and live in response to this love and grace?

Though your role is to lead or facilitate the group, you are not on your own. Through the book *All the Good: A Wesleyan Way of Christmas* and the accompanying DVD, four Wesleyan scholars and pastors will serve as your guides, helping you and your group come to a deeper understanding of what it means to respond to the love of God in Christ in a Wesleyan way.

In addition to the book and video segments, you have this leader guide, which provides all you will need for implementing four meaningful group sessions. It's likely that you have more than enough material in these pages, so feel free to choose from the options in the "Learning Together" sections to fit the time allotted for your group meetings.

Each participant should plan on bringing a Bible and a copy of *All the Good* to each session. If possible, notify those interested in the study in advance of the first session and make arrangements for them to obtain their books so they can read the introduction and chapter 1 before the first group meeting.

Using This Guide with Your Group

This leader guide is designed to give you options and flexibility in planning your sessions. You are encouraged to develop your sessions with your group in mind, because different groups have different interests as well as different dynamics. Choose any or all of the activities. Adapt. Reorder. Rearrange. Innovate. Make it your own to meet the particular needs of your group.

The session plans in this leader guide are designed to be completed in about 60 to 90 minutes, but you can choose fewer activities to reduce the time to 45 minutes if desired. Special preparation may be needed for some of the activities, which is indicated in the "Planning the Session" section.

Here is an overview of the session format:

Planning the Session
Session Goals
Scriptural Foundation
Special Preparation

Getting Started
Opening Activity
Opening Prayer

Learning Together
Video Study and Discussion
Book and Bible Study and Discussion

Wrapping Up
Closing Activity
Closing Prayer

Two Optional Elements

In addition to the elements you choose for your weekly session, there are two additional elements that you might find beneficial. Though they are optional, you are invited to consider how journaling and participating in your church's service and missions opportunities might enhance your group's study experience.

JOURNALING

Journaling is a wonderful way to encourage more individual reflection and more extensive interaction outside the group sessions. You can promote the use of a journal by using one of your own as part of your preparation and class time. Group members can use any sort of book they would like for journaling, from a composition book to a bound, blank journal to sheets of loose-leaf paper. Some groups might even choose to use dedicated internet sites where they can post ideas and share thoughts. That approach will give

---

you a permanent record of what you have learned and where you still have questions. Offer encouragement to those who decide to use a journal to reflect on the weekly reading, write questions for future learning, record insights during the group session, and consider commitments they might make for their own spiritual growth.

PARTICIPATE IN YOUR CHURCH'S SERVICE AND MISSIONS OPPORTUNITIES

All the Good is about responding to God's love in Jesus Christ through acts of piety and mercy—good works or means of grace. Invite group members to take part in the service and missions opportunities of your faith community during this season of Advent. Coordinate with your church leaders to develop a list of these opportunities, and consider participating in one or more of the activities not only as individuals but also as a group.

In addition to ongoing service and missions opportunities, many faith communities have particular service and missions opportunities they sponsor or support each year during Advent. As you make your way through this study, you may find that group members have a deeper appreciation for these opportunities and want to participate more fully. Your group may even want to develop their own service opportunity—whether a one-time activity or an ongoing ministry. Encourage and allow participants to determine what they would like to do as a way of responding to God's love by practicing love.

Helpful Hints

PREPARING FOR THE SESSION

- Pray for God's guidance as you lead this study. Pray, as well, for the members of your group.
- Before each session, familiarize yourself with the content. Read the book chapter and the key scriptures in the chapter. Take your time, savoring every word. If you can, read more than one translation.

- Depending on the length of time you have available for group meetings, you may or may not have time to do all the activities. Select the activities in advance that will work for your group time and interests.
- Choose the session elements you will use during the group session, including the specific discussion questions you plan to cover. Be prepared, however, to adjust the session as group members interact and questions arise.
- Have your own sense of how you might respond to the questions, and if you are uncertain or wrestle with any of them, admit this to the group. This will give participants permission to wrestle and question themselves.
- Prepare the room where the group will meet so the space will enhance the learning process. Ideally, group members should be seated around a table or in a circle or semicircle so that all can see one another. Movable chairs are best because the group will sometimes be forming pairs or small groups for discussion.
- Bring a supply of Bibles for those who forget to bring their own.
- For most sessions you also will need a whiteboard and markers, or an easel with large sheets of paper and markers.

Shaping the Learning Environment

- Begin and end on time.
- Create a climate of openness, encouraging group members to participate as they feel comfortable.
- Not all members of the group may know one another. Even if people do know one another, have them introduce themselves. They might share a joy or concern or one way they typically respond to God's love in Christ during Advent and Christmas (some activity or tradition in which they share God's love).
- Name tags can be helpful, even in groups where everyone supposedly knows one another.

- Remember that some people will jump right in with answers and comments, while others need time to process what is being discussed.

- If you notice that some group members are not entering the conversation, ask them if they have thoughts to share. Give everyone a chance to talk, but keep the conversation moving. Moderate to prevent a few individuals from doing all the talking.

- Communicate the importance of group discussions and group exercises.

- If no one answers at first during discussions, do not be afraid of silence. Count silently to ten, and then say something such as, "Would anyone like to go first?" If no one responds, venture an answer yourself and ask for comments.

- Model openness as you share with the group. Group members will follow your example. If you limit your sharing to a surface level, others will follow suit.

- You might share some questions of your own to acknowledge that you do not know everything or have all of the answers.

- Encourage multiple answers or responses before moving on. Rather than asking, "What does this mean?" ask, "What does this mean *to you*?" Assure participants that there may be more than one good answer to a question, just as there is more than one way to tell the story of Jesus's birth.

- To help continue a discussion and give it greater depth, ask, "Why?" or "Why do you believe that?" or "Can you say more about that?"

- Affirm others' responses with comments such as "Great" or "Thanks" or "Good insight," especially if it's the first time someone has spoken during the group session.

- Monitor your own contributions. If you are doing most of the talking, back off so that you do not train the group to listen rather than speak up.

- Remember that you are not expected to have all the answers but to encourage participation and keep the discussion going.

MANAGING THE SESSION

- Honor the time schedule. If a session is running longer than expected, get consensus from the group before continuing beyond the agreed-upon ending time.
- Involve group members in various aspects of the group session, such as saying prayers or reading the Scripture.
- Note that the session guides sometimes call for breaking into smaller groups or pairs. This gives everyone a chance to speak and participate fully. Mix up the groups from week to week to prevent the same people from pairing up for every activity.
- As always in discussions that may involve personal sharing, confidentiality is essential. Group members should never pass along stories that have been shared in the group. Remind the group members at each session that confidentiality is crucial to a good group experience.

Session 1

Practicing Advent
Preparing the Way

LACEYE WARNER

Planning the Session

SESSION GOALS

As a result of this session, group members will begin to

- reflect on John the Baptist's call to "prepare the way of the Lord" (Matthew 3:3),
- reflect on the meaning of the Advent season through the lens of John Wesley's practices of the "means of grace,"
- consider three roles or aspects of God's grace (prevenient, justifying, and sanctifying),
- understand that the "means of grace" are ways to connect with God and one another through good works in response to God's love and grace,

- learn the difference between works of piety and works of mercy,
- appreciate that good works do not earn God's grace but are a response in gratitude to God's love, and
- Consider how small groups help us grow in holiness of heart and life.

Scriptural Foundation

> *In the fifteenth year of the reign of Emperor Tiberius, when Pontius Pilate was governor of Judea, and Herod was ruler of Galilee, and his brother Philip ruler of the region of Ituraea and Trachonitis, and Lysanias ruler of Abilene, during the high priesthood of Annas and Caiaphas, the word of God came to John son of Zechariah in the wilderness. He went into all the region around the Jordan, proclaiming a baptism of repentance for the forgiveness of sins, as it is written in the book of the words of the prophet Isaiah,*
>
> > *"The voice of one crying out in the wilderness:*
> > *'Prepare the way of the Lord,*
> > > *make his paths straight.*
> > *Every valley shall be filled,*
> > > *and every mountain and hill shall be made low,*
> > *and the crooked shall be made straight,*
> > > *and the rough ways made smooth;*
> > > *and all flesh shall see the salvation of God.'"*
>
> *John said to the crowds that came out to be baptized by him, "You brood of vipers! Who warned you to flee from the wrath to come? Bear fruits worthy of repentance.*
>
> *Luke 3:1-8a*

Special Preparation

- If you are not in a room with a large table, prepare the room with seating arranged in a circle so that everyone will be able to see one another.

- Have name tags available, as well as pens and markers for the tags.
- Have available a whiteboard or large sheet of paper with markers for writing. Prepare for the "Opening Activity" by writing the heading "Preparing for Christmas" on the board or paper.
- Provide Bibles for those who may not have brought one. Encourage participants to bring a Bible for future sessions. Let participants know that they can bring whatever Bible version they prefer; sometimes it is helpful to share and read from different translations.
- Gather information on the practices of the Examen and journaling to share with group members, or create a simple handout with links to share.[1] (*optional*)
- Write the Prayer of Saint Francis on a whiteboard or large sheet of paper, or create a handout for the group for the "Closing Prayer." (See page 44.)

Getting Started

OPENING ACTIVITY

As participants arrive, greet them and invite them into a circle of chairs or to the table. Especially if you are working with a newly formed group, have each of the participants write his or her name on a name tag and put it on. Begin the session with brief introductions.

Tell the group that this study will explore how we can anticipate, receive, and respond to God's amazing love embodied in Jesus Christ in a "Wesleyan way"—a way that recognizes we do not earn God's love but accept it and respond to it by practicing love through holiness of heart and life. These loving practices of piety and mercy, or good works, are often referred to as means of grace. In these four sessions, we will reflect on biblical passages and Wesleyan themes in light of various means of grace, considering what it means to (1) practice Advent, or prepare the way for

God's love in Christ; (2) practice prayer; (3) practice mercy and care for others; and (4) practice God's mission to the world.

Ask group members to share ways they prepare for Christmas, when we celebrate the coming of Christ into the world. You can start them off with an example, such as "putting up a Christmas tree," "buying presents," or "attending worship services." As participants share, write their responses on a whiteboard or large piece of paper with the heading "Preparing for Christmas." Save the list for reference during the "Closing Activity."

OPENING PRAYER

Lead the group in prayer using the following prayer or one of your own choosing:

Good and loving God, Advent is a time when we prepare to receive your presence in the birth of Jesus Christ, who embodies your love for all creation. Help us to respond to your amazing gift by loving you and loving others. Remind us what it means to practice Advent and participate in your love and grace. Amen.

Learning Together

VIDEO STUDY AND DISCUSSION

Play the first track on the DVD, *All the Good*, Session 1: Practicing Advent: Preparing the Way (running time is 11:22).

After the video session plays, invite discussion and questions from the group. To spark conversation, ask group members to consider the following excerpts from the video session and the questions that follow:

Excerpt 1:

> The story of John the Baptist has always appealed to me
> with its "ready or not, here I come" ethos—the theme
> of "I'm in the wilderness, and I'm coming out to tell you
> that Jesus is coming, that the Son of God is on his way."

And so that spirit of "ready or not, here I come" that we pick up on in the children's game hide-and-seek is that we no longer need to hide. But God is always seeking for us. And in Advent we experience that most fully as we read the Advent stories and wait for the arrival of Jesus, "God with us," on Christmas day.

- How does Advent remind us that we no longer need to hide from God?
- In what ways do the stories and rituals of Advent help you realize and experience the reality that God is seeking you?

Excerpt 2:

As we choose God, we realize that we are choosing joy and flourishing and thriving and grace. And we know the depth of that gift because we also know what it is to be without God. That mystery [of God giving us the option to sin] is really a part of the gift so that we can experience choice—experience bad choices yet at the same time experience that most amazing choice, that all we need to do is to receive being loved by God.

- How does our freedom to choose sin enable us to also experience the joy and grace that come from choosing God? How has choosing God brought joy and grace into your own life?
- Why do we often resist being loved by God? How can we choose to receive God's love—during Advent and throughout the year?

Excerpt 3:

[Authentic sharing in community] is tremendous risk and tremendous vulnerability, but in that participation with God and the Holy Spirit, God can bring us to a place that is really within the beauty of the reign of God, even in the midst of pain and difficulties.

- What hinders and what facilitates authenticity and vulnerability in community?
- How have you experienced the beauty of the reign of God through vulnerable and authentic sharing in community?

BOOK AND BIBLE STUDY AND DISCUSSION

Choose from the following talking points and questions. More material is provided than you likely will have time to cover, so select those questions you wish to include in your session, identifying them with a check mark. Excerpts from the book *All the Good* appear within quotation marks.

John the Baptist Prepares the Way

- Have someone read aloud Luke 3:1-7 (see pages 18–19). How did John prepare the way of Jesus? What did he call people to do, and why?

- "Throughout biblical texts the same story unfolds repeatedly in different scenes with a range of characters. . . . Humanity sins. God invites relationship, offering forgiveness and salvation. Advent represents the climax of this story line. God sends the ultimate invitation in Jesus Christ, fully human and fully divine, born into the world to inaugurate God's reign and redeem all of creation from the power of sin and death."

  ◊ Why is it important for us to recognize Advent as the climax of the story line of God's desire to redeem all of creation from the power of sin and death?

  ◊ What does it mean for us to respond to God's invitation in Jesus Christ "with love"?

  ◊ John Wesley suggested that we express love by cultivating "fruits meet for repentance" through good works or means of grace. Do you see any correlation between this idea and John the Baptist's words in John 3:8a? Why or why not?

God's Grace

- Have group members turn to Psalm 51. When you read this psalm, what stands out to you more—David's sinfulness or God's grace? Why do you think this is so? How can we see God's gracious goodness in this psalm?
- "Instead of focusing on God's grace for all creation, we focus on contrasting ourselves with one another, highlighting degrees of sinfulness. Or we engage in a related but equally destructive tendency: we compete with one another for worldly favor, measuring accomplishments."
  - ◊ Why do you think we are inclined to focus more on sin—comparing degrees of sinfulness and competing for worldly favor and accomplishments—than on God's grace? How might we become more grace-centered in relationship to God and neighbor?
- Share the following summaries aloud:

Some would say that John Wesley viewed grace as "God's presence and power to save and transform individuals, societies, and the whole of creation." Faith in response to grace is the only requirement for salvation. Christian practices are a response to God's justifying grace and a means of receiving or experiencing God's sanctifying grace.

"Prevenient grace goes before, preceding human effort or response. It is universally present, prompting, convicting, wooing, and preparing us to accept God's invitation into relationship."

"Justifying grace is God's presence to forgive, save, and reconcile us to God and one another."

"Sanctifying grace is God's presence and power, through the Holy Spirit, to form and shape us in the image of

Christ, perfect us in love, and create in us 'holiness of heart and life.'"

◊ How do these understandings of grace help us avoid works righteousness, which is earning our right standing with God through good works?

Small Groups and Accountability

• The vitality of the early Methodist movement was due in large part to small group gatherings. John Wesley believed that authentic spiritual formation was not possible "without society, without living and conversing with [others]."[2] There were two kinds of groups, and all members followed three general rules:

Classes: 10–12 participants organized geographically (Today we might call them community groups.)
Bands: 6–8 participants organized around a common experience. (Today we might call them affinity groups, organized by age, gender, and/or marital status.)

Three General Rules:
1. Do no harm, and avoid every kind of evil.
2. Do good.
3. Attend upon the ordinances of God—including the means of grace or works of piety and mercy.

◊ How are these two types of groups similar to and different from the groups we see in faith communities today, including your own faith community?
◊ Do you think contemporary small groups might benefit from the kind of accountability provided by the three General Rules? If so, what might that look like, practically speaking?

Works of Piety and Mercy

- "Wesley divided the means of grace into two groups: works of piety and works of mercy (or charity)." Works of piety nurture an individual's spiritual growth, and works of mercy address the bodies and souls of others. (Share the examples below.) Wesley prioritized works of mercy because of the perception that they are more difficult to practice.

  Works of piety—prayer, confession, the Lord's Supper, Scripture study and meditation, fasting, praise and worship, keeping a diary (journaling)
  Works of mercy—selfless service (feeding the hungry, clothing the naked, entertaining the stranger, visiting the sick/imprisoned/afflicted), evangelism, discipleship of others

  ◊ Do you agree with Wesley that works of mercy are more difficult to practice than works of piety? Why or why not?
  ◊ What are the advantages or benefits of encouraging or incorporating works of piety and mercy within small groups? How might we do that today—or how have you seen it done?
  ◊ Wesley organized educational opportunities, medical dispensaries, and microlending resources to help impoverished people live sustainably. What are some ways that today's faith communities are involved in helping to shape responses to systems of oppressive poverty?
  ◊ Why is Advent an appropriate time to begin or renew practices of the means of grace?

- "Practicing the means of grace is similar to tending a garden. The gardener prepares the soil, distributes water, plants seeds, and daily supports the seeds through germination, growth, and fruit. However, the gardener does not have the power to create the seed, sunlight, or water, or to cause it to grow and produce fruit.... The miracle of the seed, its growth, and its fruit, come from God."

◊ How would you complete this gardening analogy in terms of what happens when we read or study biblical texts, pray, worship, and serve others?

Care of Time

- "John Wesley learned early in his spiritual journey the importance of one's use of time as a daily discipline." He used a diary to document the use of his time, noting his "temper" during each activity on a scale of 1 to 9 and using as many as twenty questions to guide the evaluation of his daily activities.

  ◊ Though Wesley's particular process of recording his daily activities and rating his emotional states during those activities may seem stringent to us, how might reflecting on our daily experiences help us grow in holiness of heart and life? What spiritual practices could be helpful in this kind of daily or regular examination? (*Optional*: Provide information on the Examen and journaling. See "Special Preparation.")

- One of the outcomes of daily practicing means of grace is increased honesty between ourselves and God. In the light of such honesty, evil forces have less room to grow as God's grace heals our brokenness.

  ◊ What spiritual practices are part of your daily or regular routine (or which ones would you like to be)? How have these practices fostered honesty and authenticity in your relationship with God? How have they brought healing for your brokenness?

- Mary McLeod Bethune—the first African American to establish a four-year institution of higher learning, founded a national organization to lobby the federal government, and held the high-level government appointment of director of the Negro Division of the National Youth Administration—attributed her success to her Christian faith, including simple daily spiritual practices.

◊ How have daily or regular spiritual practices helped you (or someone you respect) to "put feet to your faith"? How have they impacted your (or their) relationships, work, and influence?

Wrapping Up

CLOSING ACTIVITY

Divide into groups of two or three and share your responses to the following questions:

• What is your hope for your relationship with God? What are three ways in which you can cultivate that relationship? (Refer to the list of Christmas preparations created during the opening activity. After today's discussion, is there anything you now wish to add to the list?

CLOSING PRAYER

Come back together as a full group, and read aloud the Prayer of Saint Francis as your closing benediction. In advance, write the prayer on a whiteboard or large sheet of paper, or create a handout for the group.

Lord, make me an instrument of Your peace:
where there is hatred, let me sow love;
where there is injury, pardon;
where there is doubt, faith;
where there is despair, hope;
where there is darkness, light;
where there is sadness, joy.

O, Divine Master, grant that I may not so much seek
to be consoled as to console;
to be understood as to understand;
to be loved as to love.
For it is in giving that we receive,
it is in pardoning that we are pardoned,
and it is in dying that we are born again to eternal life.
Amen.

Session 2

Praying in Advent

SANGWOO KIM

Planning the Session

SESSION GOALS

As a result of this session, group members will begin to:

- reflect on Luke 1 and Zechariah's prophecy of Jesus Christ's birth;
- consider how the story of Christ's incarnation can enrich their understanding of prayer and Christian life;
- understand that prayer is about cultivating a loving relationship with God, experiencing unity or oneness with God, and being transformed by participation in the divine nature;
- consider their own practices of prayer during the season of Advent;
- explore what it means to pray continually; and
- cultivate an openness to receive God's love and vision for their lives.

Scriptural Foundation

"Blessed be the Lord God of Israel,
*   for he has looked favorably on his people and redeemed them.*
He has raised up a mighty savior for us
*   in the house of his servant David,*
as he spoke through the mouth of his holy prophets from of old,
*   that we would be saved from our enemies and from the*
*   hand of all who hate us.*
Thus he has shown the mercy promised to our ancestors,
*   and has remembered his holy covenant,*
the oath that he swore to our ancestor Abraham,
*   to grant us that we, being rescued from the hands of our enemies,*
might serve him without fear, in holiness and righteousness
*   before him all our days.*
And you, child, will be called the prophet of the Most High;
*   for you will go before the Lord to prepare his ways,*
to give knowledge of salvation to his people
*   by the forgiveness of their sins.*
By the tender mercy of our God,
*   the dawn from on high will break upon us,*
to give light to those who sit in darkness and in the shadow of death,
*   to guide our feet into the way of peace."*

Luke 1:68-79

Special Preparation

- Prepare the room with seating arranged in a circle or around a table so that everyone will be able to see one another.
- Have name tags for all returning as well as new members.
- Have available a whiteboard or large sheet of paper with markers for writing. Prepare for the "Opening Activity" by writing the heading "Prayer is…" on the board or paper.
- Provide Bibles for those who may not have brought one.

Getting Started

OPENING ACTIVITY

As participants arrive, greet them and invite them into a circle of chairs or to the table. Especially if you are working with a newly formed group, have each of the participants write his or her name on a name tag and put it on.

In advance, write on a whiteboard or large sheet of paper "Prayer is…" Begin by having group members introduce themselves again and, as they do, have each person complete the statement "Prayer is…" without repeating what has been said previously by others in the group. Save the list for reference at the end of the session.

OPENING PRAYER

Lead the group in prayer using the following prayer or one of your own choosing:

God of love, you emptied yourself of all but love to become a human and make us like you. Help us understand that because of the Incarnation, we can seek perfect union with you through prayer. Transform us as you transform our understanding and our experience of prayer. May we come to realize that it's all about an intimate, loving relationship with you. Amen.

Learning Together

VIDEO STUDY AND DISCUSSION

Play the second track on the DVD, *All the Good*, Session 2: Praying in Advent (running time is 11:42).

After the video session plays, invite discussion and questions from the group. To spark conversation, ask group members to consider the following excerpts from the video session and the questions that follow:

Excerpt 1

> Prayer makes our vessel deeper and wider so [that] when [the] Holy Spirit pours out blessings upon us, we can receive them well. In prayer we are shaped and reshaped, becoming more like Jesus; and in our love we become more and more ready to serve other people. And in that way I think prayer makes us ready to be engaging God and engaging other people around us.

- How does the idea that our prayers make us deeper and wider vessels for the blessings of God enrich your view of prayer?
- How has prayer helped to shape and reshape you to become more like Jesus? How has it moved you toward love and service of God and neighbor?

Excerpt 2

> What kind of language we choose, what kind of petitions we bring to God (or what kind of petitions we do not bring to God), and also how we use our bodies in our conversations with God—all of these together reveal a lot about ourselves and our understanding of God.

- What do your personal prayers reveal about your understanding of yourself, others, and God?
- What do the public prayers of your faith community reveal about your communal understanding of self, others, and God?

Excerpt 3

> I trust that it is not my prayer, my words, and my worthiness but it is the grace of God [that] makes my prayer more acceptable and beautiful in the eyes of God. God is already working in my prayer. God speaks to me, and Jesus speaks for us, and the Holy Spirit prays for

us in our prayers. And I find this mysterious work of
Trinity really beautiful in my prayer.

- Does it encourage you to know that it is the grace of God,
  not your words or your worthiness, that makes your prayers
  acceptable and beautiful in the eyes of God? Explain your
  response.
- What does it mean to say that God is already working in our
  prayers? How is each person of the Trinity at work in prayer?

BOOK AND BIBLE STUDY AND DISCUSSION

Choose from the following talking points and questions. More material
is provided than you likely will have time to cover, so select those questions
you wish to include in your session, identifying them with a check mark.
Excerpts from the book *All the Good* appear within quotation marks.

Prayer and Advent

- Many of us were not taught how to pray. "If we are interested in
  sustaining a prayerful life, we need more structured support and
  practice." The liturgical seasons of the church year help to locate
  our stories in Jesus's story (his birth, baptism, ministry, teaching,
  transfiguration, suffering, death, resurrection, ascension, sending
  of the Holy Spirit, and the promised second coming). By
  following the liturgical calendar, our prayer lives are shaped and
  reshaped in the story of Christ.
  - ◊ How do the liturgical seasons help you connect with Jesus
    and his story? What is your favorite season of the church
    year, and why?
  - ◊ How has the season of Advent, in particular, helped to shape
    or influence your Christian life, including your prayers?

- Most of us have a genuine desire to pray, yet we have trouble
  praying consistently for a variety of reasons—our prayers seem
  to hit a wall, our requests are not granted, we don't hear God,

we're afraid of what God might ask of us; we feel vulnerable and exposed, we uncover the depths of our hearts (which can be overwhelming and disorienting); we are excited and/or afraid of our growing intimacy with God, and so on.

◊ Which of these hindrances to prayer do you relate to most? What has kept you from praying consistently? Has there ever been a time when you stopped talking to God, giving God the silent treatment? If so, share briefly about that time as you are comfortable.

◊ Read aloud Matthew 26:36-46. How did Jesus also struggle in prayer, and how does this speak to all of humanity's struggle with prayer?

◊ If all human beings struggle in prayer and God already knows our needs better than we do, why do we still need to bring our petitions to God?

• Read aloud Romans 8:34 and Romans 8:26. Then share the following: "Those who pray are incorporated into Christ, who is in unity with God the Father. We never come to God as an absolute other; instead, we find ourselves in the mysterious work of the Trinity, who is both the speaker and listener of prayer. In our voices, God the Father hears the voice of the interceding Christ. Our prayer is not our own accomplishment but rather God's gift of grace coming through the Holy Spirit, who frees, enables, and incites us to pray. When we cannot find words for prayer, the Holy Spirit also 'intercedes with sighs too deep' for human language."

◊ How does prayer involve us in the mysterious work of the Trinity? How would you explain what happens when we pray?

◊ How does understanding prayer as participation in the circular movement of the love of God increase your hope and trust in God?

Zechariah's Prophetic Song

- Summarize the story of Zechariah and Elizabeth (see Luke 1 and pages 50–54 in *All the Good*). Then read out loud Zechariah's song, found in Luke 1:68-79 (see "Scriptural Foundation" on page 28).

   ◊ What do you imagine this old, childless couple talked, prayed, and dreamed about before the angel's announcement to Zechariah? What do you imagine Elizabeth and Mary talked, prayed, and dreamed about in their three months together?

   ◊ Why is Zechariah's song a song of prophecy? How does it make a connection between what God had already begun and what God would fulfill?

   ◊ What is significant about the reference to "the hand of the Lord," and how does this connect with what happens in prayer? How do we "hold hands" with God and others in prayer?

   ◊ How is Zechariah's prayer both human speech and the inspired words of God? Likewise, how are our prayers not only our words but also God's words given to us, and what role does the Holy Spirit play in this?

- Zechariah's reference to "the dawn from on high" represents Christ, and early Christians prayed toward the east, the direction of the sunrise, in anticipation of Jesus's promised second coming. "Zechariah's song…has been a principal part of the church's traditional daily morning prayer. With the Song of Mary, or *Magnificat* (Luke 1:46-55), in evening prayer and the Song of Simeon, *Nunc Dimittis* (Luke 2:29-32), in night prayer, Luke's three canticles on Jesus's birth are staples of the daily liturgy of the church."

   ◊ How might the symbolism of Jesus as "the dawn from on high" inspire your own prayer habits or postures?

◊   Why do you think these three songs about Jesus's birth have become staples of the daily liturgy of the church? How might reflecting on Jesus's coming enrich your own prayers—not only at Advent but also throughout the year?

Learning How to Pray

- Like the songs of Zechariah, Mary, and Simeon, "the Psalms and canticles in the Bible have been a backbone of Christian prayer in both communal liturgy and private devotion. They passionately express the whole gamut of emotions, including joy, sorrow, anger, fear, and surprise."
  ◊   How have the psalms helped you discover your own emotions and learn to express your heart? If you have a favorite psalm or psalms you turn to in prayer, share briefly about why they resonate with you.

- "Learning how to pray is like learning a different language; it involves acquiring a different view of God, self, church, and world. We can learn how to pray by borrowing words from the church's prayers: the Lord's Prayer, Psalms, canticles, and liturgy. Those borrowed words become ours, and they eventually become who we are."
  ◊   How has prayer been like learning a different language for you? How has it helped you acquire a different view of God, yourself, others, and the world?
  ◊   Which prayers of the church have become your own prayers? How have they shaped who you are?

- Prayer is like a school for spiritual and emotional growth. John Wesley explained the transformation that happens in prayer this way:

  The end of your praying is not to inform God, as though he knew not your wants already; but rather to inform yourselves; to fix the sense of those wants more deeply in your hearts, and the sense of your continual dependence on him who only is able to supply all your wants. It is not so much to move God…as to move yourselves, that you may be willing and ready to receive the good things he has prepared for you. (John Wesley, "Sermon on the Mount, VI")

◊   How has prayer brought spiritual and emotional growth in your life?

◊   What is your response to the idea that prayer is more about moving yourself than moving God? When has prayer helped you to be willing and ready to receive what God has planned for you?

• "Words eventually fail us.… Silence does not replace our words in prayer, but silent prayer begins where our words crumble. In silence, we open ourselves to God's presence and listen to the voices of the triune God mysteriously working in our prayer."

◊   How does silence help us to become aware of God's presence and hear God's voice?

◊   How have you incorporated, or how would you like to incorporate, silence into your times of prayer? What questions or challenges come to mind when you consider silent prayer?

John Wesley and Prayer

• "Wesley's vision of prayerful life had two wings: the rubric of prayer books, which gave a structure to the life of holiness, and fervent extempore prayer, which allowed…spontaneous, often explosive, outpourings of emotions. Wesley envisioned that our spiritual growth would be support by both wings, but his Methodists quickly lost the first wing, mostly relying on the second one only."

◊   Do you agree with Wesley that both formal written prayers and spontaneous prayers are essential to a vital life of prayer? Why or why not?

35

◊ What role has each kind of prayer (formal and spontaneous) played in your life of faith?

◊ What types of prayer are most common in your faith community?

- In Emily Brontë's novel *Wuthering Heights*, Heathcliff is described as "praying like a Methodist." Noting that his voice became hoarse, we can assume Brontë was referring to the wailing and shouting characteristic of the Methodist practice of fervent prayer in nineteenth-century England. This emotive prayer often was accompanied by physical movement, such as kneeling, falling down, and dancing.

  ◊ How would you describe what it means to "pray like a Methodist" today?

  ◊ Regardless of our style of prayer, how can prayer become prayer of the heart—prayer that helps us shape our desires and character and that brings about our sanctification?

- To Wesley, Christian perfection was not perfection in knowledge or freedom from temptation but more like "being in the zone with the Holy Spirit." We might say that it is "a life so saturated in love that all our thoughts and actions are overflow from love." The author points out that "prayer has a unique place in our journey toward entire sanctification. Prayer is not only the means of grace that leads us toward perfection, but in union with God we live in perfection itself."

  ◊ If Christian perfection is "being in the zone with the Holy Spirit" or being "saturated in love," how might prayer help to move us toward this goal?

  ◊ What role has prayer played in your own sanctification process? How has it influenced your life in the Spirit and your experience of connection with or union with God?

- Read aloud 1 Thessalonians 5:16-18.
  - ◊ How are rejoicing, praying continually, and giving thanks interconnected? What outcome did Wesley believe these practices would bring in an individual's life?
  - ◊ What can help us to move from viewing prayer as an intermittent action to viewing it as constant communication with God?
  - ◊ How can the metaphor of prayer as "the breath of spiritual life" inform and inspire our understanding of prayer?

- In his treatise "The Character of a Methodist," Wesley "explained that the distinguishing 'marks of a Methodist' were…their commitment to spiritual discipline and their transformed hearts filled with love of God and love of neighbor. He named praying without ceasing as one of those marks." For Wesley, true prayer was an unspoken language of the heart.
  - ◊ What does it mean to say that prayer is an unspoken language of the heart? Practically speaking, how can we "speak" this language in our daily lives?
  - ◊ How might our love for God and neighbor be a barometer of our prayer lives—an indication of our practice of praying without ceasing?

Incarnation and Sanctification

- "Christ made our sanctification possible, not only by empowering us to do the right things but also restoring our human nature itself. By becoming a human being, Christ opened the possibility for us to be like him." John Wesley wrote this about the divine nature:

> By salvation I mean…a present deliverance from sin, a restoration of the soul to its primitive health, its original purity; a recovery of the divine nature…. This implies all holy and heavenly tempers, and by consequence all holiness of conversation.[1]

◊ How does knowing that Christ came not only to make God visible but also to make possible our transformation through participation in the divine nature affect your understanding of the Incarnation? How might it influence your celebration of Advent?

◊ What does it mean to you to become like Christ? On a scale from 1 to 10, with 1 being low and 10 being high, where do you fall when it comes to believing that you can partake in the divine nature and become holy? Explain your response.

• "John Wesley explained our partaking in divine nature not as something we possess but as a loving relationship with God. It is not about who we are as independent beings; it is about who we are in our relationship with God. We are drawn into 'a deep, an intimate, an uninterrupted union with God; a constant communion with the Father and his Son Jesus Christ, through the Spirit; a continual enjoyment of the Three-One God, and of all the creatures in [God]!'"[2]

◊ If our transformation results from a loving relationship with God, then how should we view prayer?

◊ How is prayer much more than communicating our wants and needs? How might it be not only a way toward perfection but also an experience of it?

Prayer and Love of Neighbor

• "We never pray alone, even when we enter a closet and pray alone in secret.... In our prayers, we are all connected to one another in the Spirit. We pray for the entire world because we care about others."

◊ How does prayer invite us to participate in God's mission and the transformation of the world? How is intercessory prayer an expression of divine love?

◊ Do you believe that prayer inspired by the Spirit of God should make us deeply engage in the world? Explain your response.

◊ How are your prayers leading you to take action in our broken world?

◊ How can remembering what Christ has done for us in Christ's incarnation, as well as what he has promised to fulfill in us, fuel our prayers and our acts of love during Advent—and throughout the year?

Wrapping Up

CLOSING ACTIVITY

Focus your attention again on the list from the opening activity. As group members look over the words, ask them to think about their ideas about prayer based on the information we've covered from chapter 2 of the study book. Would they change or add anything to the list? (Write any additional thoughts on the board or paper.) What on the list stands out most? What is God highlighting for each of them?

CLOSING PRAYER

Have group members turn to page 78 in the study book, and pray this prayer together in unison:

Love Divine, all loves excelling,
Come to our hearts, and teach us how to pray.
Hear our prayers of love.
Open our ears to hear your voice.
Help us to partake in your glory.
Transform our hearts to be made perfect in love.
Make us united with you in our prayers.
We pray in the name of Jesus, Love Incarnate, Amen.

Session 3

Practices of Mercy

Embodying God's Love for Others

JUNG CHOI

Planning the Session

As a result of this session, group members will begin to:

- reflect on Luke 1:26-56 and the obedience of Mary to follow God's call beyond her comfort and understanding;
- understand that God's vision of mercy is for everyone, especially the marginalized and the poor;
- consider John Wesley's understanding of acts of mercy and what acts of mercy look like in our world and lives today;
- recognize that responding to God's call opens us to the beauty of God's love and mercy for us and for all of creation; and
- consider how God might be calling us to respond to God's love.

SCRIPTURAL FOUNDATION

In the sixth month the angel Gabriel was sent by God to a town in Galilee called Nazareth, to a virgin engaged to a man whose name was Joseph, of the house of David. The virgin's name was Mary. And he came to her and said, "Greetings, favored one! The Lord is with you." But she was much perplexed by his words and pondered what sort of greeting this might be. The angel said to her, "Do not be afraid, Mary, for you have found favor with God. And now, you will conceive in your womb and bear a son, and you will name him Jesus. He will be great, and will be called the Son of the Most High, and the Lord God will give to him the throne of his ancestor David. He will reign over the house of Jacob forever, and of his kingdom there will be no end." Mary said to the angel, "How can this be, since I am a virgin?" The angel said to her, "The Holy Spirit will come upon you, and the power of the Most High will overshadow you; therefore the child to be born will be holy; he will be called Son of God. And now, your relative Elizabeth in her old age has also conceived a son; and this is the sixth month for her who was said to be barren. For nothing will be impossible with God." Then Mary said, "Here am I, the servant of the Lord; let it be with me according to your word." Then the angel departed from her.

In those days Mary set out and went with haste to a Judean town in the hill country, where she entered the house of Zechariah and greeted Elizabeth. When Elizabeth heard Mary's greeting, the child leaped in her womb. And Elizabeth was filled with the Holy Spirit and exclaimed with a loud cry, "Blessed are you among women, and blessed is the fruit of your womb. And why has this happened to me, that the mother of my Lord comes to me? For as soon as I heard the sound of your greeting, the child in my womb leaped for joy. And blessed is she who believed that there would be a fulfillment of what was spoken to her by the Lord."

And Mary said,

"My soul magnifies the Lord,
*   and my spirit rejoices in God my Savior,*
for he has looked with favor on the lowliness of his servant.
*   Surely, from now on all generations will call me blessed;*
for the Mighty One has done great things for me,
*   and holy is his name.*
His mercy is for those who fear him
*   from generation to generation.*
He has shown strength with his arm;
*   he has scattered the proud in the thoughts of their hearts.*
He has brought down the powerful from their thrones,
*   and lifted up the lowly;*
he has filled the hungry with good things,
*   and sent the rich away empty.*
He has helped his servant Israel,
*   in remembrance of his mercy,*
according to the promise he made to our ancestors,
*   to Abraham and to his descendants forever."*

And Mary remained with her about three months and then
returned to her home.

Luke 1:26-56

Special Preparation

- Prepare the room with seating arranged in a circle or around a table so that everyone will be able to see one another.
- Have name tags for all returning as well as new members.
- Have available a whiteboard or large sheet of paper with markers for writing.
- Provide Bibles for those who may not have brought one.

Getting Started

Opening Activity

As participants arrive, greet them and invite them into a circle of chairs or to the table. Especially if you are working with a newly formed group, have each of the participants write his or her name on a name tag and put it on.

Invite each group member to share one way he or she is involved in practicing mercy (meeting the needs of others) or working for justice in the world. List them on a whiteboard or large piece of paper.

OPENING PRAYER

Lead the group in prayer using the following prayer or one of your own choosing:

Almighty and merciful God, thank you for this time to study with others and learn more about what it means to practice mercy. Open our hearts to your vision for the world through Mary's story and song. Like Mary, may we be filled with praise and choose bold obedience, joining you in your vision to transform the world through Christ. Amen.

Learning Together

VIDEO STUDY AND DISCUSSION

Play the third track on the DVD, *All the Good*, Session 3: Practices of Mercy: Embodying God's Love for Others (running time is 11:39).

After the video session plays, invite discussion and questions from the group. To spark conversation, ask group members to consider the following excerpts from the video session and the questions that follow:

Excerpt 1

It's really important for us to remember that in our Christian life, God's agency and human agencies are all mingled. It is not like that we are just passively receiving [God's grace]...we are practicing our obedience [in a] very active way. And I think this is fierceness and this is boldness; and in our obedience—which is, of course,

44

humility and which is also faithfulness—we are actively receiving [God's grace] and we are actively thankful for God's grace in our lives. And we are actively practicing this love for others.

- What does it mean to say that God's agency and human agency are mingled or intertwined? How have you experienced this mystery in your own life?
- How is obedience to God more than passive receptivity or acceptance? When and how have you been fierce and bold in your obedience to God's will and grace?
- What does it mean to be actively thankful? How has God's love moved you to practice love for others?

Excerpt 2

When we gather together to study the Bible together and we think critically and honestly with one another—and, of course, there is vulnerability when we share...then we realize that the beauty and the essence of Christianity is for us always to think that it is not us who are in the center, but it is God who is in the center.... We may be wrong in our understanding, but we are trying to do God's work in God's name with one another.... When we hear from one another,...trying to listen to people's stories and how they have made their relationship with God stronger and how they have matured in their relationship with God (what we call sanctification), we can learn...so that we can become mature.

- How does being in community help you remember that it is God who is in the center, not us?

- How has listening to the wisdom and stories of others in the body of Christ—through small group study and discussion as well as personal sharing—helped you mature in your faith and relationship with God?
- Do you believe sanctification is possible outside of Christian community? Explain your response.

Excerpt 3

> It is important to see that it was not just Mary; Mary had Elizabeth. And they were going through similar— not the same, similar—situations together. And that was such an important way to bolster one another.... If it is only one, we may think that we are not sure whether this is God's call to me, whether I heard it right. But when we have our companions, our sisters and brothers and siblings in Christ, we can discern together, "OK, they have gone through a similar way. I can do this as well. Things may be hard, but we can do this together."

- When it comes to being obedient to God, what can we learn from Mary's example?
- When we are discerning God's invitations and calls in our lives, especially when they are outside of others' expectations, how can our brothers and sisters in Christ help us? How have others helped you in your own times of wrestling with discernment and obedience?

BOOK AND BIBLE STUDY AND DISCUSSION

Choose from the following talking points and questions. More material is provided than you likely will have time to cover, so select those questions you wish to include in your session, identifying them with a check mark. Excerpts from the book *All the Good* appear within quotation marks.

God's Agency and Mary's Obedience

- Read aloud Luke 1:26-56 (see "Scriptural Foundation," pages 42–43). In Mary's story and song, we see both God's incredible power, which saves people through all time, and Mary's obedience in response to God's amazing power. "God's will and power could be perceived as violent, for … God's breaking in Mary's life forever changed her life." Yet we see that Mary is not a passive recipient but an active participant. She says yes to God, proclaiming, "Here am I, the servant of the Lord; let it be with me according to your word" (Luke 1:38).
  - ◊ How do we see both God's agency and Mary's agency in Mary's story and song? In her song, specifically verses 46-55, what is the evidence for God's saving power, and what is the evidence of her willing obedience?
  - ◊ Has God ever broken into your life in a surprising way, forever changing your life? If so, share briefly about that experience and your response.

- "Mary's obedience and faithfulness serve as a model.… This fierce and bold obedience must have come from her relationship with God, her trust in God, who leads and takes care of God's people as God promised."
  - ◊ In what ways was Mary's obedience "fierce" and "bold"?
  - ◊ Read aloud Luke 11:27-28. How does Jesus's response to the woman in the crowd show us that Mary was blessed by her obedience and relationship with God rather than by the biological birth of Jesus? How does this encourage us?

Magnificat: God's Vision for the Marginalized and Poor

- Mary's song, the *Magnificat*, offers a prophetic vision "connected to God's mercy on everyone, especially on the marginalized, the lowly, and the poor." This vision of the great act of mercy that would break barriers and spread God's justice and liberation for

all people was not just a dream for the future but was fulfilled
with Jesus coming into the world, because Jesus ministered to the
lowly and exalted the humble.

◊   Read aloud Luke 6:20 and Matthew 5:3. How do these
    verses add nuance to Mary's vision in the *Magnificat*?

◊   How is Mary's vision of mercy evident today? How do we see
    God's mercy and salvation here and now in our world? How
    are God's mercy and salvation evident in *your* life right now,
    in this season of Advent?

Mary's Communal Vision for All

*   "Mary's song is inextricably connected to many years of the
    Israelites' history and emphasizes the loving relationship
    between God and human beings, and God's promise to deliver
    God's people from evil. Mary's song is a form of prophecy—as
    John Wesley also pointed out with many other theologians[1]—
    which was connected to the history of Israel, through various
    prophets who prophesy for God's desire for the world, and most
    important, for Christ's salvation."

    ◊   Read aloud Hannah's song in 1 Samuel 2:1-10 and
        Zechariah's prophecy in Luke 1:67-79. How do both
        Hannah and Zechariah respond to God's call in a similar way
        to Mary's song? How do they glorify the amazing work of
        the Lord?

    ◊   How have other prophets and poets throughout the ages
        helped us to see the mysterious work of God, which involves
        us yet is beyond our understanding? Who has helped you to
        better understand the mysterious work of God?

    ◊   When and how have you been a participant in the mysterious
        work of God? What comes to mind first?

*   John Wesley tells us in his Explanatory Notes that "Mary said,
    under a prophetic impulse, several things, which perhaps she
    herself did not then fully understand." In other words, Mary

likely did not get the full scope of God's vision, which was for all people, not just her people. In his Gospel and the Acts of the Apostles, Luke presents Jesus as "the fulfillment of God's promise and covenant, not just for Abraham and his descendants, but also for all the people who will be blessed by Abraham (Genesis 22:18)."

◊ Read aloud Luke 2:10. According to the angel, for whom did Jesus come?

◊ Why is it important for us to recognize that Mary's full understanding was not necessary for the fulfillment of God's vision for the world? Have you ever allowed your limitations to discourage you from answering God's call and doing God's work? If so, what happened?

◊ When have you seen God's vision from your own perspective instead of God's perspective in relation to other people? How can we overcome our limitations to understand God's vision?

John Wesley and God's Vision for All People

• In his sermon "The Scripture Way of Salvation," John Wesley described the "works of mercy" or "practices of mercy" necessary for full sanctification:

10. Secondly, all works of mercy; whether they relate to the bodies or souls of men; such as feeding the hungry, clothing the naked, entertaining the stranger, visiting those that are in prison, or sick, or variously afflicted; such as the endeavouring to instruct the ignorant, to awaken the stupid sinner, to quicken the lukewarm, to confirm the wavering, to comfort the feeble-minded, to succour the tempted, or contribute in any manner to the saving of souls from death. This is the repentance, and these the "fruits meet for repentance," which are necessary to full sanctification. This is the way wherein God hath appointed His children to wait for complete salvation.[2]

◊ How would you "translate" these works of mercy for our day and time? (Write the group members' responses on a whiteboard or large sheet of paper—next to the list generated in the Opening Activity.)

◊ How have you seen individuals and groups living out the vision of the *Magnificat* and Wesley's "works of mercy" in our church and community and world?

- Remind group members of the author's testimony by reading aloud the following excerpt:

When I got the calling of God's voice in my heart and answered God's calling to teach and raise future pastors for God, I was a seventeen-year-old with bright eyes.... I remember my prayers when I responded to the small voice in my heart. I recognize that it was God with whom I had had a trusting relationship. I was pleased and happy that God called me. My obedience was bold, and I was thinking, *I can go anywhere God leads me. Let your will be done in my life.* Oh, how I didn't know what kinds of journey God would lead me on. God has broken my plans so many times. I figuratively found myself on the cliff many times and cried out to God, "I thought that you called out to me to do your work. But why are things this hard? I feel like I am drowning. Where are you? Did I really hear your voice?"

In those moments, I remember Mary, who may have cried out to God countless times. "Didn't you call me? Where are you? Didn't I hear your voice? Didn't I see your presence?" But after a moment of silence, I also remember her agency, bold obedience again and again. "Let your will be done." I also feel connected to A. Carroll, M. Knowles, and Lucy Cunningim, who were American Methodist pioneers. I feel connected to my great-grandfather and my grandmothers, who were Korean Methodist pioneers. I can imagine their cries out to God. How hard it must have been for the American Methodist pioneers to be in another, foreign land and go through difficulties. I can imagine my great-grandfather who left his hometown to take the position of chaplain in the Lucy Girls' school to educate future generations of women leaders and to educate bright young girls such as my grandmothers. I also imagine so many nameless saints throughout time and space, who boldly said to God, "Yes, I can. Yes, your will be done." Their lives have been ravaged and hard and in ways they would never have imagined. Their histories and their testimonies are here with all of us.

◊ What resonates with you in this personal testimony? When have you questioned God's call in your own life? How has recalling the lives of known pioneers of faith and nameless saints encouraged and emboldened you?

Humility in Practices of Mercy

- "Our God…calls us to spread God's mercy and justice, as Mary's *Magnificat* extols and as Jesus would live out later."
    - ◊ How does Mary's song upend the worldly understanding of social structure? How is it bad news for those who try to keep the class system and status quo?
    - ◊ How do we sometimes marginalize people when trying to practice mercy, making them "less than" us?
    - ◊ Why is it important to deliver Christ's gospel within the cultural context of the people we are serving? How can we know when reconciliation and forgiveness are necessary?
    - ◊ Why is humility essential in all that we do when practicing mercy?

Advent: Fear, Longing, and Hope

- As we wait and long for the birth of Christ in Advent, our fears and hopes are intertwined. The message of God's power through even our small obedience brings forth God's greatest gifts for the world. "We encounter our God in the midst of our hope and fear, just as Mary did, and just as Jesus's disciples did. Through our encounter with God, God takes care of our fear, nourishes our hope, and gives the message in our lips and hearts so that we may cry out God's message to the world that Jesus, who is always with us, is born."

◊ How is God calling you in this season? What fears or limitations threaten to keep you from bold obedience? How can you say yes to God despite them?

◊ How has God met you in your fear in the past? What nourishes your hope?

◊ In what ways can you practice mercy this Advent?

Wrapping Up

CLOSING ACTIVITY

Divide into groups of two or three and share your responses to the following questions:

• What dreams and hopes of yours is God breaking now? What dreams and hopes is God breathing in you now?

CLOSING PRAYER

Offer the following prayer or one of your own:

Good and all-powerful God, thank you for choosing us, just as you chose Mary, to participate in bringing mercy to all people in your name. Even though we do not have full understanding and sometimes misunderstand your vision, help us to trust and follow you in bold obedience. We place our hope in you and rejoice in Jesus, the Savior of the world. Amen.

Session 4

Christmas Is Only the Beginning
God Sends the Church to the World

AMY VALDEZ BARKER

Planning the Session

SESSION GOALS

As a result of this session, group members will begin to:

- reflect on the story of the birth of Christ in Luke 2 ,
- examine how God has invited us to respond to the messenger and message by doing all the good we can in God's creation,
- consider what it means for God to perfect us in love,
- explore some of the ways we can share God's love, and
- understand that God invites all to share in God's mission with Jesus Christ to the world.

SCRIPTURAL FOUNDATION

> *In those days a decree went out from Emperor Augustus that all the world should be registered. This was the first registration*

and was taken while Quirinius was governor of Syria. All went to their own towns to be registered. Joseph also went from the town of Nazareth in Galilee to Judea, to the city of David called Bethlehem, because he was descended from the house and family of David. He went to be registered with Mary, to whom he was engaged and who was expecting a child. While they were there, the time came for her to deliver her child. And she gave birth to her firstborn son and wrapped him in bands of cloth, and laid him in a manger, because there was no place for them in the inn.

In that region there were shepherds living in the fields, keeping watch over their flock by night. Then an angel of the Lord stood before them, and the glory of the Lord shone around them, and they were terrified. But the angel said to them, "Do not be afraid; for see—I am bringing you good news of great joy for all the people: to you is born this day in the city of David a Savior, who is the Messiah, the Lord. This will be a sign for you: you will find a child wrapped in bands of cloth and lying in a manger." And suddenly there was with the angel a multitude of the heavenly host, praising God and saying,

> *"Glory to God in the highest heaven,*
>   *and on earth peace among those whom he favors!"*

When the angels had left them and gone into heaven, the shepherds said to one another, "Let us go now to Bethlehem and see this thing that has taken place, which the Lord has made known to us." So they went with haste and found Mary and Joseph, and the child lying in the manger. When they saw this, they made known what had been told them about this child; and all who heard it were amazed at what the shepherds told them. But Mary treasured all these words and pondered them in her heart. The shepherds returned, glorifying and praising God for all they had heard and seen, as it had been told them.

Luke 2:1-20

SPECIAL PREPARATION

- Prepare the room with seating arranged in a circle or around a table so that everyone will be able to see one another.
- Have name tags for all returning as well as new members.
- Have available a whiteboard or large sheet of paper with markers for writing. Prepare for the "Opening Activity" by writing the headings "Messengers of God in the Bible" and "Messengers of God in My Life" in two columns on the board or paper.
- Provide Bibles for those who may not have brought one.
- In advance, write the Closing Prayer on a white board or large sheet of paper (see pages 125–26).

Getting Started

OPENING ACTIVITY

As participants arrive, greet them and invite them into a circle of chairs or to the table. Especially if you are working with a newly formed group, have each of the participants write his or her name on a name tag and put it on.

Invite each group member to name either a messenger of God in his or her own life or a messenger of God in the Bible, adding each to the lists prepared above, and sharing briefly how that person has influenced the group member to do good and share God's love. Then talk briefly together about the defining character attributes of those listed, writing them below the respective lists. What similarities do you notice between the two lists?

OPENING PRAYER

Read the following prayer aloud, or use one of your own:

Creator God, every year we tell the story of the birth of Jesus as a reminder of who we are and to whom we belong. Jesus is the embodiment of your love, which is the foundation of our Christian faith. Jesus is your message that calls us to action. Open our hearts to hear and respond to that message anew today. Amen.

Learning Together

VIDEO STUDY AND DISCUSSION

Play the fourth track on the DVD, *All the Good*, Session 4: Christmas Is Only the Beginning (running time is 11:45).

After the video session plays, invite discussion and questions from the group. To spark conversation, ask group members to consider the following excerpts from the video session and the questions that follow:

Excerpt 1

> As people who come from a Wesleyan understanding of Christianity, we have this understanding of the means of grace and this journey toward sanctification, and for me it's always been about this journey into a deeper relationship with God and to understanding God's full divine love. And because of this full divine love, we have this draw, this calling, this desire to be part of the work that God is doing in this world.

- What are some of the ways you have felt drawn or called to be part of the work that God is doing in the world?
- How have these means of grace or good works deepened your relationship with God and your understanding of God's love?

Excerpt 2

> I think it's both that desire and that response and that enjoyment of getting to be full participants of God's work in this world that each and every one of us has the opportunity to be a part of, whether it be participating in God's work through loving our neighbor, whether it

be participating in God's work through loving our family members. All of the different ways in which God invites us to do good and be good in this world are part of what it means to be truly participants of God's work in this world today.

- How would you explain what it means to be a full participant in God's work in the world? How are we "doing good" whenever we are loving others?
- Why is it important to recognize that doing good is a response to God's love rather than a way of earning God's love?

Excerpt 3

Our responsibility is to be open to the Holy Spirit's nudges when we may be called to be the messenger for someone. But I think it's also our responsibility as participants in God's work and as receivers of God's grace to also be open when God needs us to hear a certain message. I think that's what the Christmas story is all about. In that moment around Christmas, we are so open, ready to receive that new life and that new birth.

- When have you been called to be a messenger for someone? When have you been the one receiving the message?
- Why is Advent a time when God is calling all of us to be open, ready to receive and respond?
- How is God inviting you this Advent not only to receive the story of Christmas but also to respond to it?

BIBLE STUDY AND DISCUSSION

Choose from the following talking points and questions. More material is provided than you likely will have time to cover, so select those questions you wish to include in your session, identifying them with a check mark. Excerpts from the book *All the Good* appear within quotation marks.

Messenger, Message, and Response

- The Bible is filled with stories of messengers called by God to deliver a message intended to bring God's creation back into alignment with God. "From Abraham and Isaac to David and Goliath, to Ruth and Naomi or even Esther, there is a messenger in each story, a message that God needs delivered to God's creation, and an invitation to action that is an expected response from God's people. The author of Luke most frequently puts the Holy Spirit as the central influencer in the Jesus narrative."

  ◊ Read aloud Genesis 1:1-3. How is the Spirit of God hovering over the waters a messenger of God in the story of creation? What does this reveal to us about the role of a messenger to be a catalyst, putting things in motion?

  ◊ Have someone read aloud Luke 1:35 and Luke 2:1-20. How do we see the Holy Spirit at work through the message of the angels in these passages? In each instance, how was the message of the angel a catalyst for the actions that followed?

- John Wesley views the Spirit as the "immediate cause of all holiness in us; enlightening our understandings, rectifying our wills and affections, renewing our natures, uniting our persons to Christ,"[1] "as both instigator and sustainer of the good that is inherently a part of us as the created ones. The Holy Spirit goes before us, within us, and beyond us as the messenger, the message, and the catalyst for the actions given to us by the will of God."

  ◊ Do John Wesley's views of the Spirit affirm, expand, or challenge your own views of the Spirit? Explain your response.

  ◊ How has the Holy Spirit been God's messenger, message, and catalyst for action in your life? In other words, how has the Spirit guided you, inspired you, and reminded you that God's desire is your participation in working and serving for the good of the world?

- "Recent heroes who have been messengers through the power of the Holy Spirit have been leaders such as Mother Teresa, Martin Luther King Jr., and even missionaries like E. Stanley Jones. These leaders opened their hearts and minds to submit to the power of God's Spirit in their lives, even to the point of death.... In their biographies, we read that each one of them battled their egocentric nature, allowing themselves to be vessels for the work of the Spirit."

  ◊ Who are the leaders who have modeled for you how to bravely and confidently trust the Spirit to guide and inspire you? In what ways have they allowed themselves to be vessels for the work of the Spirit? How have they been messengers preparing the way for God's message?

  ◊ Read aloud Mark 13:8-11. How do these verses show us the importance of allowing the Spirit to deliver the message that has been inspired and formed within us by God for a particular group of people? What happens when we do not trust in the Holy Spirit to speak and work through us?

The Message Is Jesus

- "Everything about Advent points to the Message, Jesus.... The message of Jesus, the Christ child, conveys the intention God has for all of God's creation through the Incarnation. When we remember this message each year at Advent, we are reminded about the foundation of our faith. We are invited to hold on to the promise of eternal life through God's love for us."

  ◊ What are the ways you remember and celebrate the message of Jesus at Advent?

  ◊ The author writes that as we get further from the initial revelation of a message, our memories begin to fade and the exciting moment is replaced with busyness. How does the excitement of Advent and Christmas begin to fade and give way to busyness in your life? What helps you to keep the

message of Jesus alive in your life, not only during Advent
but also throughout the rest of the year?

- In John Wesley's "Plain Account of Christian Perfection," he
  makes the case that the entire message of Jesus is love. And in
  his sermon "Circumcision of the Heart," he reminds us that
  Jesus said love is the fulfillment of the law—"not only the first
  and great command, but all the commandments in one." Wesley
  called the great commandment—which is to love God with all
  our hearts and souls and minds and strength—the "royal law of
  heaven and earth."[2]
  ◊ How does Jesus help us understand the heart of God's
    message? Do you agree with Wesley that the entire message
    of Jesus is love? Why or why not?
  ◊ How is love the fulfillment of all the commandments?

A Message That Leads to Action

- "Usually, messages have a purpose. The message God sent
  through Jesus, the Son of God, had a very distinctive call to
  action. The Christmas message is not merely a passive story for
  people to feel good about the moment, although many in our
  Christian communities today act as if that is the sole and whole
  purpose of Advent. This is a message…with a real purpose to
  inspire humanity and implore us to see that our actions need
  to change."
  ◊ How does your faith community view and communicate the
    message of Advent?
  ◊ In your own words, how would you express the distinctive
    call to action within the message sent by God through Jesus?
  ◊ Why was and is this message needed?

- This Advent call to action (to act differently, think differently,
  and live differently) "is not offered to earn a position with
  God.…Methodists do not believe that we can earn our way

to heaven by doing good deeds.... We do not believe that
each good decision, good word, or good action will result in
God loving us more.... The actions we offer stem from the
overwhelming power of love. Not because we expect anything
in return. Our gift of salvation has already been given to us, so
our actions stem out of our love for all of God's creation and all
of God's world. Therefore, Methodists are actively engaged in
transforming the world through actions that are often for the
greater good."

◊ Is this understanding of our response to God's gift of love
what you were taught in your formative faith community
or family? If so, what has helped you receive and respond
to the overwhelming power of God's love? If not, what has
helped or is helping you move from a more transactional
relationship with God to a relationship grounded in grace
and love?

◊ Where and how have you seen those who follow the
Wesleyan way improving communities through their
actions—both locally and around the world?

• In his sermon "The First Fruits of the Spirit," Wesley wrote:

They now "walk after the Spirit," both in their hearts and lives.
They are taught of him to love God and their neighbour, with
a love which is as "a well of water, springing up into everlasting
life." And by him they are led into every holy desire, into every
divine and heavenly temper, till every thought which arises in
their heart is holiness unto the Lord.[3]

◊ How have the loving actions of others been a "well of water"
for you throughout your life? What "amazing grace actions"
have made a significant difference in your life?

◊ How are you actively involved in sharing God's love and
participating in God's mission in the world?

Perfected in Love

- The idea of "Christian perfection" is about being "perfected in love," as Wesley put it. Unfortunately, Western culture has distorted the idea of "perfect love" into an idealistic image, and for many the term "Christian perfection" seems to suggest that we have to live life perfectly, without mistakes or sin. But being "perfected in love" means that, more and more, "our actions are primarily oriented toward the agape love God planted in our hearts at the beginning of Creation." In other words, the message of Jesus brings us to a salvific response that moves our hearts and our actions toward love. Loving God and neighbor is the most perfect way we can live because of what God has done through Jesus.

  ◊ What are some examples of the ways our culture has distorted the idea of "perfect love," and how do you think that has influenced our understanding of "Christian perfection"?

  ◊ Why is it important for those of us who follow the Wesleyan way to reclaim and embrace the concept of "Christian perfection"? How might this increase our hope and vision for a better future where we are both actors in the transformation of a broken world and recipients of that transformation?

  ◊ What would it look like for *you* to lean in to being "perfected in love"? How does the message of Jesus move your heart and your actions toward love? How is welcoming the Creator into the world through the Christ child this Advent helping to move you toward agape love?

- "Every year we are told the story of the birth of Jesus as a reminder of who we are and to whom we belong.... This identity as Christian people is our defining *WHY* our presence in the world matters. It is the practice time we need as we move back into the world, sharing God's love and God's grace with everyone we meet.... Through the beauty of the message, and the gift of the Holy Spirit, we move into the world renewed" to do all the good we can, in all the places we can.

◊ How does the message of Advent serve as the foundation of our faith?

◊ How might viewing Advent as "practice time" for moving into the world to share God's love and grace deepen your experience of the season?

◊ What would help to encourage you and hold you accountable to do "all the good you can" throughout the year?

Wrapping Up

CLOSING ACTIVITY

Sing together (or have someone read aloud) all three verses of the hymn "Hark! The Herald Angels Sing" (*United Methodist Hymnal*, no. 240). Then briefly discuss the following questions:

- How does this hymn convey the full message of Jesus?
- How does it call us to respond?

CLOSING PRAYER

Direct group members' attention to the whiteboard or large sheet of paper where you've written the following closing prayer (write the first part of the prayer in one color, and the second part of the prayer, which appears in boldface below, in another color). Explain that you will read the first part of the prayer and they are to join you in reading the second part in unison.

Loving, Creator God, thank you for opening our eyes to the wonder of your Creation and the magnitude of your love embodied in Jesus Christ. **Our desire is to respond to your love by being vessels of your transforming love and grace, bringing healing in this broken world this Advent season and throughout the year. Amen.**

Notes

Session 1

1. A few online resources include:

    Joe Iovino, "Praying the Examen: Following Jesus in Our Daily Lives," UMC.org, August 22, 2018, https://www.umc.org/en/content/praying-the-examen-following -jesus-in-our-daily-lives;
    "The Daily Examen," IgnatianSpirituality.com, https://www.ignatianspirituality .com/ignatian-prayer/the-examen/;
    Barbara Bruce, "Journal Your Thoughts," Ministry Matters, August 30, 2014, https://www.ministrymatters.com/all/entry/5379/journal-your-thoughts;
    David Lawrence, "Keeping a Spiritual Journal," The Methodist Church website, https://www.methodist.org.uk/media/5027/dd-explore-devotion-keeping-a -spiritual-journal-0313.pdf.
2. Sermon 24, "Sermon on the Mount IV," i.1, *Works* 1:533–34, referred to in Randy L. Maddox, "Formation for Christian Leadership: Wesleyan Reflections," Summary of Proceedings (American Theological Library Association) 57 (2003):124. Available online at https://hdl.handle.net/10161/7896.

Session 2

1. John Wesley "Farther Appeal," pt. I, §3
2. John Wesley, Sermon, "New Creation."

Session 3

1. With many other theologians, John Wesley considered Mary's Song as a prophecy. He said, "[Mary] speaks prophetically what was already done, which God was about to do by the Messiah. He hath scattered the proud—visible and invisible." John Wesley, Explanatory Notes upon the New Testament. By John Wesley, M.A. Late Fellow of Lincoln-College, Oxford, vol. 1 (Philadelphia: Joseph Crukshank, 1791), Evans Early Imprint Collection, https://quod.lib.umich.edu/e/evans /N18482.0001.001/1:3.3.1.1?rgn=div4;view=fulltext, v. 51.
2. John Wesley, "Scripture Way of Salvation," pt. 3, no. 10.

Session 4

1. Thomas Jackson, ed., T*he Works of John Wesley*, 14 vols. (Grand Rapids: Baker Book House, 1979), 10:82.
2. John Wesley, "Christian Perfection," CCEL website, accessed June 17, 2021, https://ccel.org/ccel/wesley/perfection/perfection.ii.i.html.
3. John Wesley, "The First Fruits of the Spirit: Sermon 8," The Museum of Methodism & John Wesley's House, accessed June 17, 2021, https://www.wesleysheritage.org .uk/exhibits/john-wesleys-sermons/sermon-sheet/?o=2667&t=.